Dear Participant:

Thank you for attending CCAR's Recovery Coaching [...]
our flagship training, the CCAR Recovery Coach Academy©. This curriculum provides a basic and introductory version of recovery coaching in order to meet the needs of those who want a general understanding of the recovery process to better understand and support the recovery of their loved ones, friends, and colleagues. Although we believe our five-day curriculum is the preferred vehicle to learn about this very important role, we do realize that not everyone has the desire to become a recovery coach or the amount of time need for that type of endeavor.

Our hope is that many of your questions about recovery and the recovery process will be answered. Much like the journey of recovery, this training provides you with an emotionally rich experience, combined with skills and techniques for real life application. Whether you use it to improve your relationships with those in or seeking recovery, or apply it to your own recovery, you will be transformed.

Participants in this course will learn to:

◊ Define & increase fluency in the language of recovery

◊ Build capacity to understand, support and advocate for recovery

◊ Learn about specific skill sets key to supporting recovery

◊ Create a learning community to advance the recognition, acceptance and support of recovery

We wish you well,

CCAR Staff

*Many of the modules contained in this work have been adapted from the nationally recognized CCAR Recovery Coach Academy©.

Contents

Agenda

Introductions
Creating a Safe Place/Working Agreements/Expectations
Three-Legged Stool
Active Listening
Spectrum of Attitudes
Discovering and Managing our Own Stuff
Exploring Addiction
Stigma
Reconnection
Stages of Change
Recovery
Stages of Recovery
Multiple Pathways of Recovery
Building Recovery Capital
Wellness
Advocacy

Working Agreement and Expectations

Working agreements are guidelines developed by a group of people regarding how they will work together to create a positive, productive process. Working agreements describe a set of desired behaviors all members of the group agree to exhibit. When creating working agreements for today, we recommend adopting these as well:

◊ A willingness to be vulnerable about your beliefs and attitudes

◊ Open-mindedness toward fellow members' beliefs and opinions as they are shared during the course

◊ A willingness to allow each person to share without fear of judgment or ridicule

◊ Enthusiastic hope that we will all complete this program wiser and more accepting than when we started

For this course, the agreed upon working agreements will be posted for reference.

The Three-Legged Stool

Much of this curriculum is based on our teachings at our nationally recognized CCAR Recovery Coach Academy©. Through the years, we have come to identify Recovery Coaching Fundamentals:

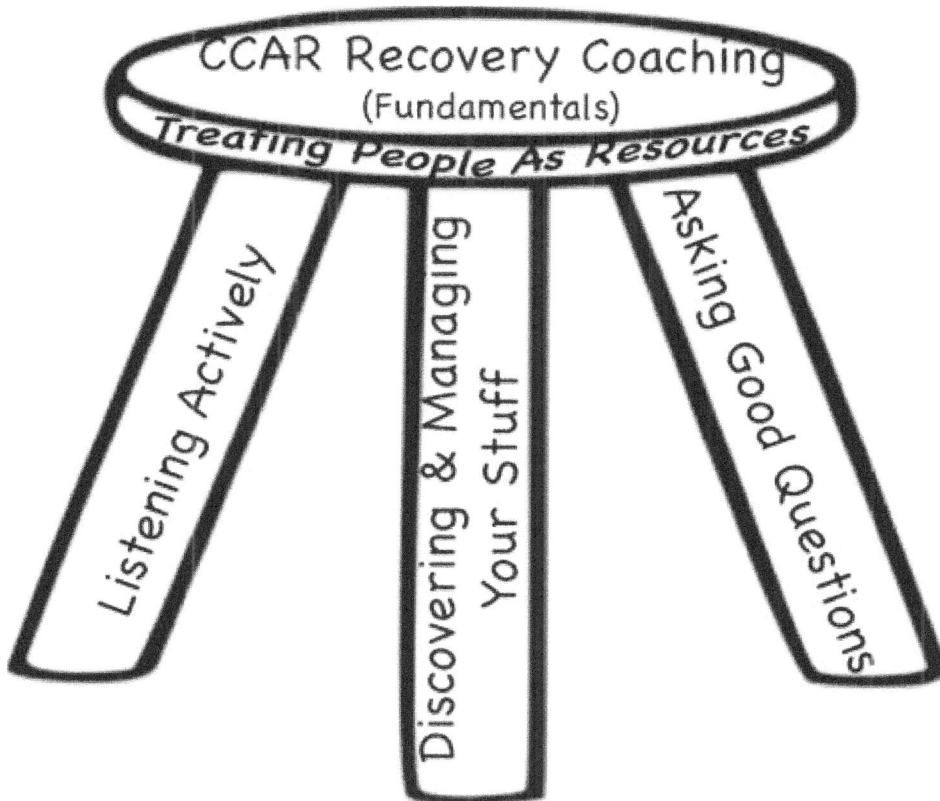

While we understand your goal is not necessarily to serve as a recovery coach, these principles can serve you well in any relationship, especially as you support someone in or seeking recovery. We will spend some time to look at these fundamentals further.

Active Listening

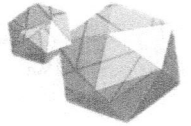

How would you describe the term active listening?

Please list the key components of active listening.

What may prevent us from actively listening?

Active Listening

Active Listening is fully concentrating on what is being said rather than just passively 'hearing' the message of the speaker. Active listening involves listening with all senses.

◊ Focus your attention on the subject (stop all non-relevant activities)

◊ Avoid distractions (a window, a talkative neighbor, noise, etc.)

◊ Seat yourself appropriately close to the speaker

◊ Acknowledge any emotional state

◊ Set aside your prejudices, your opinions

◊ Be other-directed; focus on the person communicating

◊ Follow and understand the speaker as if you were walking in his/her shoes

◊ Be aware: listen with your ears but also with your eyes and other senses

◊ Let the argument or presentation run its course; don't interrupt

◊ Be involved: actively respond to questions and directions; use your body position (e.g. lean forward) and attention to encourage the speaker and signal your interest

Remember: LISTEN and SILENT have the same letters.

Why do you think Active Listening is important?

The Spectrum of Attitudes

From *Discovering the Meaning of Prevention: A Practical Approach to Positive Change*
by William A. Lofquist

The Spectrum of Attitudes focuses on the nature and quality of relationships between and among people. The three attitudes making up the spectrum might prevail in any kind of relationship -- between parent and child, between manager and subordinate, between teacher and student, between elected officials and citizens, between husband and wife.

People Viewed as Objects

The basis of this attitude is that one person or group of people "knows what's best" for another person or group of people; or the first person or group may decide they have a right to determine the circumstances under which the second person or group will exist. The person being viewed and treated as an object usually knows it.

People Viewed as Recipients

Here the first person or group still believes they know what is best for the other, but they "give" the other the opportunity to participate in decision-making because it will be "good" for the other person or group. Thus, the other is supposed to receive the benefits of what the first person gives to them.

People Viewed as Resources

Here there is an attitude of respect by the first person or group toward what the other person or group can do. This attitude and the behaviors that follow it can be closely associated with two matters of great concern: self-esteem and productivity. Creating a culture in which people are viewed as resources is a worthy goal.

The Spectrum of Attitudes

Please think of a time you were treated as an object. What did it feel like?

Please think of a time you were treated as a recipient. What did it feel like?

Please think of a time you were treated as a resource. What did it feel like?

Asking Good Questions

In order to treat someone like a resource, we will need to ask questions. Some questions are better than others when looking for someone to share specific pieces of information. One technique that is useful is motivational interviewing. Rooted in clinical application, motivational interviewing is defined as attempting to move an individual away from a state of indecision or uncertainty and towards finding motivation to making positive decisions and accomplishing established goals.

Within Motivational Interviewing good questions are described as (OARS):

Open Ended Questions

Affirmation

Reflective Listening

Summary Reflections

Open questions invite others to "tell their story" in their own words without leading them in a specific direction. Open questions should be used often in conversation but not exclusively. Of course, when asking open questions, you must be willing to listen to the person's response.

What are some examples of open ended questions?

Affirmations are statements and gestures that recognize strengths and acknowledge behaviors that lead in the direction of positive change, no matter how big or small. Affirmations build confidence in one's ability to change. To be effective, affirmations must be genuine and congruent.

What are some examples of providing affirmations?

Asking Good Questions

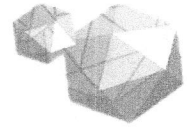

Reflective listening is the pathway for engaging others in relationships, building trust, and fostering motivation to change. There are three basic levels of reflective listening that may deepen or increase the intimacy and thereby change the affective tone of an interaction. In general, the depth should match the situation. Examples of the three levels include:

◊ Repeating or rephrasing: Listener repeats or substitutes synonyms or phrases, and stays close to what the speaker has said

◊ Paraphrasing: Listener makes a restatement in which the speaker's meaning is inferred

◊ Reflection of feeling: Listener emphasizes emotional aspects of communication through feeling statements. This is the deepest form of listening.

What are some example phrases that demonstrate reflective listening?

Summaries are special applications of reflective listening. They can be used throughout a conversation but are particularly helpful at transition points, for example, after the person has spoken about a particular topic, has recounted a personal experience, or when the encounter is nearing an end.

Summarizing helps to ensure that there is clear communication between the speaker and listener. Also, it can provide a stepping stone towards change.

What are some examples of summarizing?

Why is it helpful to ask good questions?

Discover and Manage Your Own Stuff

This is something that we are all constantly doing, and will continue to do as we help those in or seeking recovery. If we are truly going to support someone in their recovery process, we may need to check some of "our stuff" at the door.

What are some examples of "stuff" that you can think of?

A Place for Elephants

Many of us have experience with the disruptive effects of addictive behavior. For something that looms so large in our lives, it often goes unacknowledged, the elephant in the room.

Drawing on your internal and external experiences related to addiction, please take a few minutes to express your thoughts around the "elephant" in your room.

How has the elephant blocked your vision or path moving forward?

How does acknowledging the elephant (stuff) help us to move forward?

Addict vs. Addiction

Addict

Please take a few minutes to define what the word addict means to you.

_____
_____
_____
_____
_____
_____

Addiction

Please take a few minutes to define what the word addiction means to you.

_____
_____
_____
_____
_____
_____

Addict vs. Addiction

According to Merriam Webster **addict** is a very old word with a first known usage date of 1534. Dictionary.com places it in the same decade with a Latin origin that means assigned or surrendered. Feel free to write down your thoughts as you read each of the terms below:

Addict (verb): to devote or surrender oneself to something habitually or obsessively, or to cause physiologic or psychological dependency to a substance in a person or animal.

Thoughts?

Addict (noun): someone who is physiologically or psychologically dependent, who has habituated or abandoned him/herself to an activity or substance.

Thoughts?

Addiction (noun): the state of being enslaved to a habit or practice or to something that is psychologically or physically habit-forming to the point that cessation results in severe trauma, generally referred to as withdrawal.

Thoughts?

What Is Addiction?

Addiction is a disease that makes it hard to stop certain patterns and habits that increasingly interfere with a person's life. The practice could involve a substance such as alcohol or another drug, or an activity such as gambling.

Not everyone agrees about the exact meaning of addiction, but the checklists for determining if someone has an addiction usually include these items:

◊ the person cannot stop the substance use or the activity, despite trying to stop again and again

◊ the substance or the activity has become the focus (or preoccupation) of the person's life

◊ the person continues the use or activity despite severe negative consequences, (e.g., imprisonment or financial disaster).

It seems that people develop addictions through a mixture of factors such as:

◊ genes

◊ the way a person's brain works

◊ difficulties during childhood

◊ mental health problems

◊ stress

◊ cultural influences.

While researchers continue to study the mysteries of addiction, some things are clear: nobody chooses to become addicted, and addiction is not simply due to personal weakness or character flaws. It has even become acceptable to use these words casually to refer to someone who enjoys something so much he or she does it with great frequency e.g. chocoholic.

What Is Addiction?

What are your thoughts about those casual terms?

What are your reactions to addiction being classified as a disease?

What are some reactions you've heard from others?

Stigma

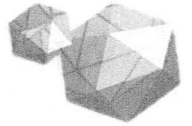

There is an abundance of stigma when it comes to addiction, which in turn prevents people from accessing services in the first place. As someone who is interested in supporting one's recovery you may be exposed to this type of stigma. You may even need to gain an understanding of the words that hurt, so that you can shed some of these labels caused by stigma from your vocabulary or to help shed it from the vocabulary of those around you.

In your small groups, please generate a list of words that you have heard to describe someone who is an addict?

Why do we label?

Stigma

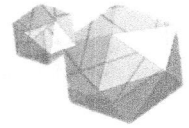

Why do we in the Recovery Community wish to eliminate the stigma that exists for those in recovery?

◊ Turns "difference" into inequity & disadvantage

◊ Maintains/upholds inequitable structures

◊ Leads to social & economic exclusion

◊ Fuels and can be used to justify violations of human rights, discriminatory policies & laws

◊ Intensifies & sustains vulnerability

◊ Impedes access to health & other services

Impact:

◊ Physical and social isolation

◊ Loss of relationships

◊ Gossip & Verbal Abuse

◊ Loss of livelihood

◊ Loss of housing

◊ Rejection by peers

◊ Loss of reputation

◊ Violence

◊ Denial or sub-standard health care

◊ Internalized stigma

Stigma

How can we help?

◊ Acknowledge the prevalence of concurrent mental health & substance use problems.

◊ Try to "walk in the shoes" of a person who is stigmatized.

◊ Watch our language.

◊ Monitor media & openly critique stigmatizing material.

◊ Respond directly to stigmatizing material with a letter to the editor.

◊ Speak up about stigma to friends, family & colleagues.

◊ Be aware of your own attitudes & judgements.

◊ Provide support for organizations that fight stigma.

We can begin by changing our language.

Example: Instead of using "addict" to "person with substance use disorder" or "person in recovery".

What are some terms we should celebrate?

My Experience with Change

Think about a change you made in your life. In the spaces below please describe the change and develop two lists – one of the supports that helped you make the change and one of the obstacles/barriers that made the change more difficult – these can be your thoughts and actions, the statements and actions of others, or simple environmental factors that existed at the time.

The change I made

_____
_____
_____
_____
_____
_____

Helps	Hindrances

Stages of Change

The Stages of Change, a model developed by Prochaska and DiClemente in 1982, is commonly used as a basis for developing effective behavior interventions. Whereas most may see the need to change a behavior as an event (quit smoking, drinking, etc.), this model shows that change is a process that goes through five stages. Change is often accompanied by supports and challenges, and by looking at the dynamics of the stages of change, we will better understand the process.

The five stages of change are:

1. Precontemplation

2. Contemplation

3. Preparation

4. Action

5. Maintenance

Stage of Change: **Precontemplation**

◊ Person shows no intent to change a problem behavior.

◊ Person may be unaware behavior is a problem, or unwilling to do anything about it.

◊ Person may lack confidence to change behavior due to previous failed attempts.

◊ Person tends to view target behavior as being more positive than negative (Decisional Balance).

◊ Person believes behavior to be under control or at least manageable.

Stage of Change: **Contemplation**

◊ Person is considering change, but has not yet initiated any change behavior.

◊ Person is considering implications and consequences of behavior.

◊ Person is visibly distressed by target behavior.

◊ Person has started to weigh the positive and negatives of the target behavior.

◊ Person will typically seek out relevant information about the target behavior.

Stages of Change

Stage of Change: **Preparation**

◊ Person is getting ready to change the behavior, both in attitude and behavior.

◊ Person intends to change soon.

◊ Person may have already started to increase self-regulation around specific behavior.

◊ Person may be prepared to make or may already be making small changes to the target behavior.

Stage of Change: **Action**

◊ Person is actively making change to target behavior.

◊ Person is modifying his/her attitudes and responses to target behavior.

◊ Person is learning skills to prevent relapse or reversal of target behavior.

◊ Action stage typically lasts an average of 6 months in people working to change substance use.

Stage of Change: **Maintenance**

◊ Person sustains and strengthens changes made to the target behavior.

◊ Person is practicing skills to prevent relapse or reversal of target behavior.

◊ Person establishes basic "habits" and "rituals" around modified behavior.

Common characteristics of people in the precontemplation stage:

◊ Defensive.

◊ Resistant to suggestions of problems associated with their drug use.

◊ Avoids steps to change drug use.

◊ Lacks awareness of the problem.

◊ Often pressured or mandated to seek treatment.

Stages of Change

Common characteristics of people in the contemplation stage:

◊ Seeking to evaluate and understand their behavior.

◊ Distressed about behavior.

◊ Desire to exert control over behavior.

◊ Thinking about making change.

◊ Have not started to make change and are not yet prepared to do so.

◊ Have made frequent attempts to change behavior in the past.

◊ Actively evaluating pros and cons of making change.

Common characteristics of people in the preparation stage:

◊ Intending to change their behavior.

◊ Ready and committed to change behavior both in attitude and behavior.

◊ On the verge of taking action.

◊ Engaged in the change process and/or treatment (TX).

Common characteristics of people in the preparation stage:

◊ Prepared to make firm commitments.

◊ Making or prepared to make decision to change.

Common characteristics of people in the action stage:

◊ Person has decided to make change.

◊ Person has made a firm commitment to change and is involved in process.

◊ Efforts to modify behavior and environment have begun.

◊ Person presents motivation and effort to achieve behavioral change.

◊ Person is willing to follow suggested strategies and activities to change behavior.

Stages of Change

Common characteristics of people in the maintenance stage:

◊ Person has made change and is working to sustain change behavior.

◊ Considerable attention is focused on avoiding relapses.

◊ Person may feel anxiety and fear around relapse and high risk situations.

◊ Person has less frequent urges to use.

◊ The last aspects of the stages of change are the tasks of the person and the coach as the recoveree moves from one stage to the next.

Precontemplation to Contemplation: Recoveree's Tasks

◊ Person must acknowledge the problem.

◊ Person must recognize the harm caused by the target behavior.

◊ Person must increase awareness of negatives of target behavior.

◊ Person should begin building confidence and self-efficacy around change in that domain.

Precontemplation to Contemplation: Coach's Role

◊ To raise doubts and increase concern and awareness around the behavior; develop hope and optimism in order to encourage consideration of change.

Contemplation to Preparation: Recoveree's Tasks:

◊ Person must make a decision to act and commitment to change behavior.

◊ Person must begin to take preliminary steps towards making change.

◊ Ambivalence around decisional balance should be resolved.

Contemplation to Preparation: Coach's Role

◊ To help the recoveree examine the impact of the target behavior and to consider the pros and cons in order to tip the decisional balance in favor of a commitment to change the target behavior.

Stages of Change

Preparation to Action: Recoveree's Tasks

◊ Person must begin to set goals and priorities to achieve change.

◊ Person must begin to develop a change plan.

◊ Person may not have stopped using alcohol and/or other drugs at this point.

◊ Change in using behavior may not occur until person reaches action stage.

Preparation to Action: Coach's Role

◊ To help the recoveree strengthen the commitment to change and help develop an action plan and strategies that facilitate the desired change to the target behavior.

Action to Maintenance: Recoveree's Task

◊ Person must apply behavior change methods and techniques for at least 6 months.

◊ Person continues to develop self-efficacy around behavior change and continually refines change behavior.

◊ Person must be actively meeting their recovery goal (i.e., abstinence: no substance use) to be considered in action stage.

Action to Maintenance: Coach's Role

◊ To support the implementation of the change plan, modifications of the plan as needed and development of new behaviors and attitudes conducive to change.

Remember that the stages of change are considered cyclical and not linear with people moving back and forth between stages.

Stages of Change

Adapted from Connors, Donovan, and DiClemente, 2001
Decelemente, 2003

Stage	Common Characteristics	Recoveree Task	Recovery Coach Role
Precontemplation ◊ No intent to change problem behavior ◊ May be unaware behavior is a problem ◊ May lack confidence to change behavior due to previous failed attempts ◊ Tends to view behavior as more positive than negative ◊ Believe behavior to be under control or at least manageable	◊ Defensive ◊ Resistant to suggestions of problems created by the addiction ◊ Uncommitted or passive in treatment ◊ Avoids steps to change use associated with the addiction ◊ Lacks awareness of the problem ◊ Often pressured or mandated to seek treatment	**Precontempation to Contemplation** ◊ Acknowledge the problem ◊ Recognize the harm caused by the addiction ◊ Increase awareness of negatives of the addiction ◊ Begin building confidence and self-efficacy	**Precontemplation to Contemplation** ◊ Raise doubts ◊ Increase concern and awareness associated with the addiction ◊ Develop hope and optimism ◊ Begin to develop discrepancy
Contemplation ◊ Considering change, has not yet initiated any change behavior ◊ Considering implications and consequences of behavior ◊ Starting to weigh the positives and negatives of the behavior ◊ Typically seeks out relevant information about the target behavior	◊ Seeking to evaluate and understand the addiction ◊ Distressed about the addiction ◊ Desire to exert control over the addiction ◊ Thinking about making change ◊ Have not started make change ◊ Not prepared to make change	**Contemplation to Preparation** ◊ Make a decision to act ◊ Commit to change ◊ Take first steps towards making change ◊ Resolve ambivalence	**Contemplation to Preparation** ◊ Examine the impact of the addiction ◊ Consider the pros and cons of addiction in order to tip the decisional balance in favor of commitment to change

Stages of Change

Adapted from Connors, Donovan, and DiClemente, 2001
Decelemente, 2003

Stage	Common Characteristics	Recoveree Task	Recovery Coach Role
Preparation ◊ Getting ready to change, both the specific behavior and attitude ◊ Intends to change soon ◊ May have already increased self-regulation around behavior ◊ May be prepared to make small changes ◊ May already be making small changes	◊ Intending to change addictive behavior ◊ Ready and committed to change ◊ On the verge of taking aciton ◊ Engaged in the change process ◊ Ready to make firm commitments	**Preparation to Action** ◊ Establish priorities ◊ Set goals for achieving change ◊ Develop a plan for change	**Preparation to Action** ◊ Strengthen the commitment to change ◊ Help develop an action plan and strategies that facilitate the desired change
Action ◊ Actively making change to target behavior ◊ Modifying attitudes and responses to behavior ◊ Learning skills to prevent relapse ◊ Action stage typically lasts an average of six (6) months in people working on an addiciton	◊ Decision to make change ◊ Firm commitment to change ◊ Involvement in process of change ◊ Efforts to change behavior and environment ◊ Motivated ◊ Willing to follow suggested strategies and activities	**Action to Maintenance** ◊ Apply behavior change methods and techniques for at least 6 months ◊ Develop self-efficacy ◊ Refine change behavior ◊ Actively meet recovery goals	**Action to Maintenance** ◊ Support the ongoing implementation and modifcation of the plan for change ◊ Support development of new behaviors and attitudes conducive to change

Stages of Change

Adapted from Connors, Donovan, and DiClemente, 2001
Decelemente, 2003

Stage	Common Characteristics	Recoveree Task	Recovery Coach Role
Maintenance ◊ Sustains and strengthens changes addressing specific behavior ◊ Practicing skills to prevent relapse ◊ Establishing basic habits and rituals around modified behavior	◊ Achieving change ◊ Working to sustain change ◊ Focus on avoiding relapse ◊ May be experiencing anxiety and fear around relapse ◊ Becoming aware of high risk situations and developing strategies to cope with them	**Maintenance** ◊ Develop routines ◊ Become aware of the positives associated with the change ◊ Practice healthy attitudes (gratitude, service, hope, encouragement, etc.)	**Maintenance** ◊ Celebrate ◊ Encourage ◊ Reinforce positives ◊ Notice the progress made by the recoveree ◊ Focus on other quality life issues

What is Recovery?

Please take a few minutes to write what recovery means to you.

Include attributes, dynamics, instances, components, etc.

_____

_____

_____

_____

_____

_____

_____

_____

_____

Recovery Core Values

People in recovery created a set of core values to advise the Connecticut Department of Mental Health and Addiction Services. People in recovery from the effects of addiction have adapted them in order to focus their own forward-facing efforts as follows:

Recovery Premise 1: All individuals are unique and have special needs, goals, health attitudes and behaviors as well as expectations for recovery.

Recovery Premise 2: Persons in recovery will have had different experiences; management of their own lives and mastery of their own futures will require different pathways at times.

Recovery Premise 3: All persons should be offered equal access to recovery and have the opportunity to participate in their recovery process.

In the recovery movement different stakeholders have expressed these premises in a number of ways. Here are two examples, the Guiding Principles of Recovery and the Ten Components of Recovery.

Guiding Principles of Recovery

Self-directed – What the person in recovery wants, desires and can accomplish; not what the provider imparts to the person

Strengths-based – Focus on strengths, capacities, talents and skills

Empowerment – Providing the tools needed to empower the person

Basic Needs – Recovery is not possible without meaning, purpose, goals, housing, work and personal development

Hope – People do recover and change is possible

Optimism – You can do it, many do

Positive Self-identity - Recovery focused, not disorders focused

Being of Service – Giving back

Recovery Core Values

Ten Components of Recovery

In 2005, a SAMHSA* Consensus Conference wrote the following ten components of recovery:

1. Self-directed

2. Individualized and Person-centered

3. Empowerment

4. Holistic

5. Non-linear

6. Strengths-based

7. Peer supported

8. Respect

9. Responsibility

10. Hope

How do you see yourself supporting these principles?

How do you think a recoveree would respond to being treated in this fashion?

*Substance Abuse & Mental Health Services Administration

CCAR's Philosophy of Recovery

A person is in recovery if they say they are.

What are your thoughts and feelings about this definition?

Can you foresee any difficulties you might have supporting this definition of recovery?

What has been your experience with other institutional definitions of recovery?

Stages of Recovery

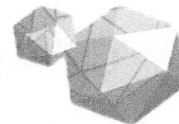

The following Stages of Recovery were modified from the work of Kathleen R. O'Connell, R.N., M.P.H., Ph.D., author of *Bruised by Life? Turn Life's Wounds into Gifts*. They offer one framework to illustrate the ongoing, progressive nature of recovery. Please review column two and create a set of parallel tasks and experiences for the affected person/parent in his or her ongoing process of recovery.

Stage	Addicts Tasks & Experiences	Affected Person's Tasks & Experiences
Stabilization **(First Year)**	**Learn** about addiction **Stay** clean & sober NMW **Physical detox** & stabilization **Learn** to socialize in a group **Learn** to break the pattern of isolation **Develop** role models for healthy recovery **Manage** anxiety **Stay away** from risky people, situations, places **Develop** self-responsibility **Learn** to ask for help & support	

Stages of Recovery

Stage	Addicts Tasks & Experiences	Affected Person's Tasks & Experiences
Deepening **(Year Two)**	**Identify** old behaviors that no longer feel right **Emotional detox** **Experience** changes in verbal attitude, feelings and behavior **Increase** physical health **Tolerate** feelings **Distinguish** between & among feeling states **Commit** to work on recovery	
Connectedness **(Years Three – Five)**	**Depth** of joy & misery can be profound **Repeat/Re-do** earlier tasks **Learn** how to stop creating drama **Manifest** inner world in outer **Connect** with a wider circle of people in and out of recovery **Increase** honesty	

Stages of Recovery

Stage	Addicts Tasks & Experiences	Affected Person's Tasks & Experiences
Integration **(Years Six – Ten)**	**Base** relationships on love vs. need **Avoid** stuck-ness **Use** recovery tools automatically **Act** on insight & knowledge **Follow through** **Forgive** oneself **Have** fun & joy in life **Practice** honesty routinely	
Fulfillment* **(Years Ten – Beyond)**	**Discover** & follow through on life purpose **Live** within an aura of peace & serenity **Reduce** worry dramatically **Accept** **Forgive** ones' self **Live** in and with fun & joy	

*The fifth stage of recovery was developed by Phil Valentine as he trained the CCAR Recovery Coach Academy© to highlight some of the characteristics of those with ten or more years of recovery.

Stages of Recovery

Did you find any parallels? Differences?

What are the implications for you as you support recovery?

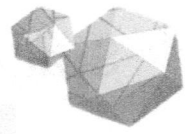

Stages of Recovery

Fulfillment

Integration

Connectedness

Deepening

Stabilization

Stages of Change

Maintenance

Action

Preparation

Contemplation

Precontemplation

Multiple Pathways of Recovery

At CCAR we honor all pathways of recovery. What works for one person may not work for anyone else. Our goal is always to provide guidance and help a recoveree find what will work best for them. This may include some pathways we may not have been exposed to, may not agree with or even disdain. In all cases, our recovery coaches need to provide guidance and mentorship in a way that is unbiased, while expanding their knowledge of programs that are unfamiliar.

Please take a few minutes to answer the following questions:

What recovery pathways are you aware of?

What pathways have you witnessed?

Are there some pathways you have found challenging? If so, why and how?

Multiple Pathways of Recovery

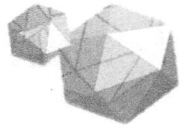

What does "the power of a personal pathway of recovery" mean to you? To the person in recovery you're supporting?

Pathways of Recovery - A Classic Framework

In an article prepared for treatment professionals and recovery advocates, William White, MA and Ernest Kurtz, Ph.D. have provided a framework for thinking about different pathways and styles of addiction recovery.

1. Scope of Recovery

◊ Primary – focuses primarily on addiction health

◊ Primary and Secondary – focuses on addiction health and global health

2. Types of Recovery

◊ Abstinence-based – Complete and sustained cessation of one's primary drug(s), the non-medical use of other psychoactive drugs and/or gambling with nicotine and caffeine historically allowed

◊ Moderation-based recovery – Sustained deceleration of alcohol and other drug use and/or gambling to a sub-clinical level, that is, a level that no longer meets diagnostic criteria

◊ Medication-assisted recovery – The use of medically monitored pharmacological drugs to support recovery from addiction

3. Context of Recovery

◊ Solo (natural) recovery – involves the use of one's own intrapersonal and interpersonal resources (family, kinship and social network) resources to resolve addiction problems without the benefit of professional treatment or involvement in a recovery support group

◊ Treatment-assisted recovery – involves the use of professional help in the initiation and stabilization of recovery

◊ Peer-assisted recovery – involves the use of structured recovery mutual aid groups to initiate and/or maintain recovery

Pathways of Recovery - A Classic Framework

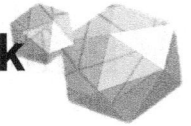

4. Recovery Framework

◊ Religious – a style in which severe addiction problems are resolved within the rubric of religious experience, religious beliefs, prescriptions for daily living, rituals of worship and support of a community of shared faith

◊ Spiritual – recovery that flows out of the human condition or wounded imperfection, involves experiences of connection with resources within and beyond self and involves a core set of values (e.g., humility, gratitude and forgiveness)

◊ Secular – a style of recovery that does not involve reliance on any religious or spiritual ideas (God or Higher Power), experiences (conversion), or rituals (prayer)

Religious and spiritual frameworks of recovery can closely co-exist and/or overlap.

5. Recovery Identity

◊ Neutral – persons who have resolved severe alcohol, other drug and/or gambling problems but do not identify themselves as alcoholics, addicts or persons in recovery

◊ Recovery-positive – those for whom the status of "recovery from addiction" has become an important part of their personal identities

◊ Recovery-negative – those whose addiction/recovery status is self-acknowledged but not shared with others due to a personal shame derived from this status

6. Recovery Terminology

◊ In Recovery – a term used to imply a way of living and/or a lifestyle

◊ Recovered – a term used to imply that a person's medical condition has been resolved

◊ Recovering – a term used to imply that recovery takes constant vigilance throughout one's life

Adapted from *The Varieties of Recovery Experience: A Primer for Addiction Treatment Professionals and Recovery Addicts* by William White, M.A. and Ernest Kurtz, Ph.D.

Multiple Pathways of Recovery

In building a toolbox of resources, take a few moments to write down some pathways you may not be familiar with, but would like to learn about after you leave the training:

Recovery Capital

Recovery Capital is the volume of internal & external assets that can be brought to bear to initiate and sustain recovery from alcohol & other drug problems.

Recovery Capital, or Recovery Capacity,

◊ Differs from individual to individual.

◊ Differs within the same individual at multiple points in time.

Interacts with an individual's problem severity to shape the intensity & duration of supports needed to achieve recovery. This interaction dictates the intensity or level of care an individual needs in terms of professional treatment. This interaction also dictates the intensity & duration of post-treatment recovery support services.

Recovery Capital is a concept linked to natural recovery, solution-focused & strengths-based helping, recovery management, resilience & protective factors & the ideas of hardiness, wellness & global health.

There are three main areas of Recovery Capital that we want to focus on:

◊ Personal

◊ Family

◊ Community

Recovery Capital

Personal Recovery Capital

- ◊ Employment
- ◊ Housing
- ◊ Clothing and Food
- ◊ Transportation
- ◊ Physical Health
- ◊ Health Insurance
- ◊ Financial Assets
- ◊ Education / Vocational skills
- ◊ Values
- ◊ Vitality
- ◊ Spirituality

Family/Social Recovery Capital

- ◊ Close Family Relationships
- ◊ Breadth of Social Relationships
- ◊ Presence of others in Recovery
- ◊ Recovery Friendly Activities
- ◊ Recovery Friendly Institutions

Where can I provide support?

Where can I provide support?

Recovery Capital

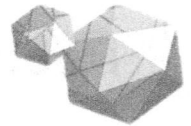

Community Recovery Capital

◊ Attitudes of Addiction/Recovery

◊ Policies regarding Addiction

◊ Access to Recovery Resources

◊ Efforts to Reduce Stigma

◊ Public Health

◊ Public Safety

◊ Quality of Life

◊ Understanding of Addiction

◊ Economic Development

Where can I provide support?

What is an Advocate?

Please take a few minutes to write a definition of the word advocate:

_____

_____

_____

_____

_____

_____

_____

_____

_____

What is an Advocate?

According to Merriam-Webster an **advocate** is one who pleads the cause of another.

How can you see yourself working as an advocate for someone in or seeking recovery?

What would I like to learn more about?

Embracing Our Elephant

Think back to this morning. We got to know each other by naming and talking about our personal experiences, what brought us here…our elephants!

The idea was to transform something that was once a liability into a gateway for helping others. Simply put, we hoped to take something unspeakable, objectionable, and all encompassing and convert its **power over us** into **power within us** to ignite our imagination and personal potential.

Imagine using the **power within us** to create change. Oftentimes it is helpful to use our stories and to share our passion for this work not only for ourselves, but to change the perceptions people might have about those who are in recovery from an addiction.

Everyone has a story…what have you learned today that would help shape your story?

_____

_____

_____

_____

_____

_____

_____

_____

_____

_____

_____

_____

_____

_____

_____

Wrap-Up Information

Thank you for your participation in the CCAR Recovery Coaching Basics©. You are among over 80,000 people who have attended CCAR training programs and have emerged a bit wiser about recovery and the individual recovery experience. While our expectation is that you will utilize the skills and knowledge gained to further your journey of becoming a recovery coach, we realize that journey, much like recovery, is different for anyone. In any case, regardless of your plans going forward, we provide these next steps to help you on your way.

Protraxx Evaluation: Upon ending your session, your facilitator will mark your attendance in the Protraxx Platform which will then send a notification to your email to complete the program evaluation. The email and link is unique to you, and you must complete the evaluation to receive your CEU Award. Due to the nature of the email, and links enclosed, the email notice may go to your spam or junk folder. If you do not receive the email, you can also check your Protraxx dashboard, the evaluation will be there for you to complete. If you do not have an evaluation to complete, please contact your facilitator directly. Once the evaluation is complete you can download you CEU award from your Protraxx Dashboard.

Things to know about your CEUs and Protraxx account:

◊ You can view your award, or save it by clicking on the "My Enrollments" tab on the menu bar.

◊ This will bring up a listing of all CCAR activities attended.

◊ You can then click on the View Award Icon.

◊ Once the award is open click the file  icon to save or print.

There is a Protraxx help page if needed here: https://addictionrecoverytraining.org/protraxx/

Recovery Coach Professional Designation: If you are interested in learning more about our CCAR Recovery Coach Professional Designation, we invite you to read, https://ccar.us/recovery-coach-professional/. For information regarding certification, please check out our certification page here: https://addictionrecoverytraining.org/certification/.

Training Opportunities: CCAR has many additional programs that build off what you have learned about the Art and Science of Recovery Coaching during the CCAR RCA. For a full calendar of upcoming events, https://addictionrecoverytraining.org/cart-events/.

Thank you for entrusting us with your professional development. Let us know how we can continue to support you.

Made in the USA
Monee, IL
31 March 2024